DIY Incc

by John Edwards

A practical guide to using UK shares, investment trusts, index funds and bonds to generate higher income returns from savings, inheritance or pension lump sum

----- for Juno, Eddie, Stan, Alex & Felix -----

Copyright © 2018 John Edwards

Disclaimer

I do not provide personal investment advice and I am not a qualified financial investment advisor. I am an amateur investor. All information found here, including any ideas, opinions, views, predictions, forecasts, suggestions, or share selection, expressed or implied herein, are **for informational or educational purposes only and should not be construed as personal investment advice.** While the information provided is believed to be accurate, it may include errors or inaccuracies. Because I am writing for a large audience, I can make no guarantees whatsoever that the information contained in this booklet will be applicable to your individual situation. I encourage you to do your own research before making any financial decision, and to seek out professional advice from an Independent Financial Adviser (IFA) if you are unsure.

Contents

1. Introduction

2. My ABC of Investing Basics
2.1 Time in the Market
2.2 Asset Allocation
2.3 Market Volatility
2.4 Diversify
2.5 Avoid High Charges
2.6 Compound Returns
2.7 The Effect of Reinvesting Dividends
2.8 Take Advantage of Tax Breaks
2.9 DYOR
2.10 An Investment Strategy Plan

3. Different Types of Investments
3.1 OEICs or Unit Trusts
3.2 Investment Trusts
3.3 Index Trackers & Exchange Traded Funds
3.4 Active -v- Passive
3.5 Shares
3.6 Bonds & Fixed Interest

4. Sustainable Income
4.1 Dividend Yield
4.2 Higher Yielding Shares
4.3 Defensive Shares
4.4 Economic Moats
4.5 Payout Ratio
4.6 Dividends Signal a Well-Run Company

4.7 Taxation Changes to Savings and Dividends

5. Set Up Your Portfolio
5.1 Selecting Your Online Broker
5.2 Comparison Sites
5.2 Selecting Your Investments
5A Individual Shares
5B Investment Trusts
5C Bonds & Fixed Interest
5D ETFs & Trackers
5E Multi-Asset Funds

6. Monitor Your Portfolio
6.1 Keeping Track of Income
6.2 Keeping Track of Capital

7. Conclusion

Introduction

This updated guide is a follow-up to my books **"DIY Simple Investing"** and **"DIY Pensions"**. I have been investing for the past 25 years and the purpose of these books is to pass on some of the knowledge I have gained over the years in what I hope is a no-frills, easy to follow approach and to help ordinary people gain some insight into the world of stocks & shares.

In my first ebook 'DIY Introduction…' I briefly covered the area of investing for income in the final chapter. However I know from the many questions on personal finance discussion boards and also in response to articles I post on my personal blog, that many people are keen to learn more about this subject in much more detail and that is what I would therefore like to address. This book is aimed at the growing numbers of people, both working families and those who may have retired, who are looking for a little more return than offered by cash deposits in recent years, not only to pay for little extras but increasingly to cover the basic costs of everyday living.

Why DIY? When I first started out in the late 1980s, shares were bought via a visit to your high street banks stockbroking department or via the telephone with one of the retail brokers in London. Research would be done via the business pages of a newspaper like the Financial Times or Telegraph - most small investors would subscribe to a weekly investment magazine such as Investors Chronicle.

Small investors now have much greater options on how and where to invest than ever before. The crucial driving force behind this has been the internet and the emergence of execution-only online brokers over the past 15 years or so. These mean that investors no longer need to call a stockbroker or use their bank in order to buy and sell investments. Instead they can access a wealth of information, research company results, view charts and performance tables and compare products available at the click of a mouse and do all this for a fraction of the cost. The rise of the DIY investing platform allows investors to access funds, shares, investment trusts, exchange traded funds (ETFs) and bonds from the comfort of their personal computer, smartphone or tablet.

The whole ethos underlying my books and blog, **diy investor (uk),** is about helping people to understand and take charge of their finances. The vested interests such as financial institutions, fund managers and advisers all benefit if investing and personal finance is regarded by ordinary people as complicated or a bit of a mystery that only the 'experts' can understand. Of course, in reality, when you break through this cloak of impenetrable financial jargon, investing can be more easily understood by anyone of average intelligence with a desire to learn.

In 2014, following the introduction of the Retail Distribution Review, financial advisers were barred from receiving commission on the products they sold and now all advisers have to charge their clients an upfront fee. The fees can range from maybe £750 up to £2,500 + vat for the initial advice plus an annual fee of typically £500 + vat for an annual review. This means that increasingly professional financial advice will be perceived as the preserve of the wealthy and many more people will be forced to go DIY.

Why Income? There's no getting away from the fact that the past decade has been tough for savers and those relying on a fixed income such as pensioners. The Bank of England reduced interest rates to a record low of 0.5% for the previous 9 years. Annuity rates are equally at an all time low and there appears little reason to think there will be any significant change for the foreseeable future.

According to a recent study by Prudential, people retiring in 2013 would receive a typical yearly income of £15,300, around £3,400 less than those who retired in 2008. In a separate report by Moneyfacts, they found that annuity income fell by 11.5% in 2012, the biggest annual fall since 1998.

Understandably, many savers are looking for alternatives which can provide a better return than the 1% or 2% currently on offer from their bank or building society. Likewise, people approaching retirement are investigating alternatives to the rock-bottom annuity rates on offer.

One way to maximise income is to invest in a diverse portfolio of large, well-run companies which will grow their earnings and profits for the decades ahead. Companies which have weathered the financial storm since the financial turmoil of 2008/09 and have also managed to maintain a steady stream of rising dividends are likely to continue doing this in the future.

Having tried many styles of investing over the years, I have come to the conclusion that the key to securing a decent return is firstly to focus on keeping costs low and secondly, to focus on the long term - for me, the next 20 years or so but certainly at least 10 years. As the saying goes, it's a marathon not a sprint.

The emphasis of this book is focussed on generating a natural income from investments, however it is equally possible to obtain 'income' from selling some of the capital that has built up from investments - this is an area I have looked at in a little more detail in my book 'DIY Simple Investing'

Why Investing? Basically, because investing over long periods of time in assets such as equities, bonds and property is likely to produce a better return than cash deposit savings in a bank or building society. I believe the biggest factors which deter most ordinary people from investing is fear and ignorance. Many people are understandably reluctant to venture into unfamiliar territory.

I hope that when the reader gets to the end of this book, any ignorance will be greatly diminished. Of course its one thing to read about a subject and sometimes a completely different thing to actually do it! I have therefore included sections on the practical 'tools' required by the small investor to get the job done and also a step-by-step guide setting out how I personally go about putting together my portfolio.

Of course, equity investing is not for everyone. Some people are temperamentally unsuited to the volatility of the stockmarket. Many people will naturally be wary of things they don't understand, others will be determined not to lose the money they have saved hard to accumulate over the years. It may be for these people there is a simple choice of cash tucked away in a cash isa with a high street bank or building society or with National Savings and that's fine. **The purpose of this book is not to persuade anyone to invest on the stock markets but merely to provide options so the individual has more information upon which a better decision can be made.**

I claim no particular originality for the contents of this guide or the methods I use to generate a little more income from my savings. All this information is widely available via the internet and accessible to anyone. I believe what can be daunting is starting from scratch and having to sift through so much unfamiliar and often conflicting information, not knowing whether to believe what you read and whether the information is accurate and authentic. The danger for the beginner is being inundated with so much information it creates an overload. My aim is to help to cut through this jungle of information and hype and focus on the basic essentials to navigate towards a sound understanding of investing for income.

All the methods described in the book have been used by me and will continue to be used for, I hope, many more years to come. Having said that, this is no 'get rich quick' book - in addition to reading the following chapters, it may take some time to research the investments to be purchased in order to build a solid portfolio which can then be left to produce years of growing tax-free income for the patient investor.

Furthermore, it will generally not be a good idea to be investing on the markets if you have outstanding debts - mortgage excepted. As I explain in my 'DIY Introduction...' book, far better to make a plan to pay off the debt(s) before even thinking of investing.

I have deliberately tried to keep this guide as simple as possible but for those who may have no previous knowledge of stocks & shares, it may well appear complex and mysterious. I have tried to avoid 'jargon' and hopefully explained the process in plain English. For further clarification on any terms which you are not familiar try www.investopedia.com

It may take several repeat readings of some sections before you begin to grasp the concept or method and translate this to your own situation. Be patient, persevere and gradually things should become clearer.

1. My ABC of Investing Basics

In my experience, investing does not need to be complicated. A pension is a long term savings plan - an ISA is a tax wrapper to keep your savings and investments out of reach of the taxman. If you pay a lot in charges for your investments you won't end up as well off in 20 or 30 years than if you paid lower charges.

This is not rocket science. You need to know a few of the basics well - the other 95% of what you come across in the financial media may be of passing interest but is generally not really necessary to make a success of diy investing.

Also, you do not need a university education to make a success of investing but you will need a plan and the ability to stick with it for a lengthy period.

Take the analogy of driving a car - you take a few lessons to learn the basics but you don't need to understand how the internal combustion engine works to get from A to B. The more journeys you make, the more relaxed and confident you become in your ability to drive the car.

In this chapter I will cover some areas of investing which should combine to provide a satisfactory outcome - provided you can exercise a degree of patience and provided you have the right temperament and can match your mix of investments with your personality.

Temperament

There is a widely held perception that investing on the stock market is very risky . I often read comments in the popular press money pages which suggest it is akin to gambling at the casino where the odds are heavily stacked in favour of the house.

There must be a good reason for this - some will result from having a poor understanding of finance generally but others may have ventured into investing without understanding the nature of the risk they were undertaking or how they would react to a sudden fall in the markets. Many new investors are sucked in to making easy money when there has been a prolonged bull market (such as early 2018 when global markets were at an all-time high!) but are totally unprepared for a 20% or 30% loss when the bull run ends and fear grips the market.

We all possess unique personality traits and preferences combined with a range of emotional biases which all impact on the way we invest - or even prevent us from engaging in the investing process completely.

A self-assessment of our emotional make-up does not need to be complicated. Most people will know whether they are naturally cautious/reserved or carefree/outgoing.

Knowing these basic types will provide some indication whether you may be better sticking with saving in a cash deposit account or, if investing for the first time, help to select the most appropriate asset mix. You can use an online tool such as Vanguard's Asset Mixer (see link) to show how various allocations of equities/bonds/cash perform over a set period.

https://www.vanguardinvestor.co.uk/investing-explained/tools/asset-mixer

Before putting our hard-earned money into stocks and shares therefore in the search for a little more income, we need to be aware of our personal capacity and reaction to any potential loss and then put in place a realistic assessment of the different assets which closely match the degree of risk and volatility we are prepared to take.

Some people are natural risk takers and may be temperamentally well suited to a higher exposure to equities when investing on the markets, whilst others are naturally cautious and require an allocation which includes less volatile assets including cash and possibly more conservative securities in the mix such as bonds, fixed interest and property.

Many people will naturally be wary of things they don't understand, others will be determined not to lose the money they have saved hard to accumulate.

For those who believe they are equiped to explore investing there are many different options and varying levels of risk and volatility. It will come as no surprise to learn that the best returns are provided by the asset class with the higher level of risk - equities and in particular individual shares; the lowest return is provided by the safest asset class - cash.

However, there are many ways to mix your allocation of the many different assets available on the market to hopefully match the degree of risk you feel most comfortable with whilst also delivering the income/return desired.

So, be sure to take it slow and steady, it's not a competition - dip a toe in the water with a conservative mix which can be adjusted as you become more experienced and get a feel for volatility.

Now turning to those basics...

In my experience, investing generally as well as investing for income, will be more rewarding if you can try to take account of the following **10 points**:

* Time in the Market

* Asset Allocation

* Market Volatility

* Diversify

* Avoid High Charges

* Compound Returns

* The Effect of Reinvesting Dividends

* Take Advantage of Tax Breaks

* DYOR - Do Your Own Research

* An Investment Strategy Plan

I will take a look at each of these in more detail

2.1 Time in the Market

The first rule of investing for me, and I'm sure many other small investors, is timeframe - the longer you have to invest, the better chances you have of riding out the long term cycles and ups and downs of the markets. You need to allow many years to have a decent chance of getting a decent return - therefore it almost goes without saying, to be successful, you should be the sort of person who is able to demonstrate a degree of patience.

If you may need your spare money for other purposes in the next 5 years - new car, holidays, new kitchen etc. then investing on the markets, however tempting, is probably best avoided. Put your spare cash in a bank or building society savings deposit account.

If you are thinking longer term - minimum 5+ years and preferably 10+ years - your investments will have a much better chance of providing better returns than your average cash deposit savings account. **I underline 'better chance' because it is important to understand that investing is all about probabilities and not guarantees.**

Better Returns from Equities Numerous academic studies over the years have shown that over the long term, investment in shares have provided a superior return to both cash and bonds. The very long term (since 1900) average for shares, after inflation, is just over 5% per year compared to under 2% for bonds and just over 1% for cash.

Equities have been the best place to invest in 6 out of the past 7 decades, however for the last decade 2000 - 2010, equities were beaten by both cash and bonds.

According to the latest Barclays Equity Gilt Study (2016), the real returns on equities (after inflation) has significantly outpaced cash savings and government bonds over 1, 5, 10, 20 and 50 years. For example, **over the past 50 years**, the real return, net of inflation and expressed as annualised % per year was:

equities 6.0%
gilts 3.1%, and
cash deposits 1.3%.

Looking at different timeframes will produce widely varying results. For example the after-inflation returns for the 10 years to end 2016 the results were -:

equities 2.5%, gilts 4.3%, and cash deposits -1.3%(negative).

As I will explain in the following chapter, the additional real return (after inflation) of 3% or 4% provided by equities over cash deposits, compounded over many years will have a significant impact. How would this translate in additional returns over, say 20 years?

As an example, lets take a lump sum of £10,000 and drip feed £100 per month over the 20 years - a total investment of **£34,000**. I have assumed a generous average rate of 3% on a cash deposit and 6.5% on equity investments (no adjustment for inflation). Using the useful calculator tools on Candid Money http://www.candidmoney.com/calculators/

the return on the cash deposit would be £50,828 and the return on the investment would be **£77,636** (after allowing for 0.5% investment charges).

Patience Be aware that these figures are based on long term averages - over shorter periods, equities may not produce the goods as we have seen for 2000 - 2010. In the Spring of 2016, the FTSE 100 dipped below 6,000 but by the end of the year and early 2017, it was above 7,200 and by early 2018 it was above 7,700 so be aware that equity investing can be a rollercoaster ride!

These are nominal figures and do not take into account dividends paid by the FTSE 100 companies - the total return figures would show a very different picture.

This is why I suggest a more realistic time frame of 10+ years. In an age of instant gratification, it can be difficult to make a long term commitment but in the words of legendary investor Warren Buffett **"The stock market is designed to transfer money from the active to the patient"**.

In the past year of 2017, the average FTSE 100 stocks and shares ISA posted a return of 11.42%, meaning an investment of £10,000 became £11,420 over the 12-month period. In comparison, the average interest rate on cash ISAs during the same period was just 1.39% – meaning a return of just £10,139 on the same investment.

Stocks and shares ISAs have provided a better return than cash ISAs 13 times in the last 17 years.

According to HMRC figures, nearly half the UK adult population has an ISA, worth an average of £16,490. Out of this, only 2.7 million adults hold a stocks and shares ISAs, compared to more than 16 million with a cash ISA.

Market Timing If you read the financial pages of the newspapers and online media, there is no shortage of opinions on where the stock markets are heading next - 'there's a bubble, the markets are due for a correction'; 'the Far East and China will drive the markets up'; 'the markets are at a five-year high and will soon go into reverse'; etc. etc.

Many small investors never make a start with their actual investing - either the markets have seen a strong surge in recent months, such as early 2018 and they are fearful there will be a correction just after they have invested their money; alternatively, the markets have sunk to new lows, there's gloom and doom around and it seems too scary to take a big risk.

The reality is that the best time to invest can only be seen in the rearview mirror i.e. in hindsight. There's probably never just the right time to invest - some say the best time is now; others say the best time is when the funds are available. My own approach was to **drip-feed** my savings into the market over a period of time, trying to take advantage of dips as I go.

The main point to make is, over the long term - 10, 20 or even 30 years, the point at which you buy an investment will become less and less important as time goes by, especially if you are reinvesting dividends to turbo-charge portfolio returns.

In the words of renowned economist JK Galbraith: 'There are two kinds of forecasters: those who don't know, and those who don't know they don't know'.

Its not so much timing the market as **time in** the market which will produce the better returns.

2.2 Asset Allocation

The usual classes of asset are equities (or shares), government bonds (gilts), corporate bonds and other fixed interest securities, commodities such as gold and silver, property and finally, cash. Asset allocation is really a question of looking at all these possible options and deciding what proportion of your investments to put in each one.

A classic allocation is 60% equities and 40% bonds. I am now in my 60s and my current allocation is 60% equities and 40% gilts, corporate bonds and fixed interest - some bonds in the form of gilts and index-linked gilts have been gradually introduced via my recent switch of some investments to Vanguard LifeStrategy index funds which hold a diverse selection of equities and bonds in a single all-in-one fund.

There is no such thing as a perfect asset allocation - each person should decide on the best mix, and of course, the mix between different classes of asset can vary over time.

One rule of thumb is to hold the same percentage of bonds as your age - so at age 30 years, it would be 70% equities and

30% bonds. At age 55 years, it would be 45% equities and 55% bonds etc.

Tim Hale, author of **"Smarter Investing"** suggests 4% in equities for each year you intend to be investing - the remainder in bonds.

Another popular choice is the Harry Browne Permanent Portfolio allocation - 25% equities, 25% gilts, 25% gold and 25% cash. The portfolio is rebalanced once per year to restore any imbalance that has arisen as one asset class does better than another.

Personally, I'm not a big fan of gold but other people will hold a significant percentage in their portfolio as a hedge against currency devaluation.

Whatever allocation you may decide is right for your investment approach, the main point is that you have addressed the issue. Also, I would not get too bogged down with 2% or 3% in this class and 4% in another - a broad brush is going to do the job and will be easier to manage and rebalance.

Many private investors start off with good intentions, but get sidetracked by the latest trend - with me it was technology shares in the late 1990s - but it could be smaller companies, emerging markets, commodities and so on. The danger is that you chop and change and end up with a dogs dinner of a portfolio.

Rebalancing   Say I choose 50% equities, 25% gilts and 25% corporate bonds - and say at the end of the year equities have done very well and have increased to 60 % of the total portfolio value. This would mean the gilts and corp. bonds represent only 40%. The idea of rebalancing is to restore the original balance of 50:25:25, therefore I sell some of my equities and reinvest the proceeds into bonds and gilts. The overall value of the portfolio has increased but the original allocation percentages are always restored at regular intervals.

Mechanics With an ever increasing choice of low cost trackers - funds and exchange traded funds (ETFs), it is relatively simple to select a range of products to provide you with a fully diversified asset allocation to fit every possible option.

Vanguard are very popular and offer a good range of equity and bond trackers (www.vanguardinvestor.co.uk). As mentioned earlier, in 2011 they introduced the increasingly popular LifeStrategy range (see under 'investment products') which combine equities and bonds in one fund according to the level of equity exposure you require - furthermore, the fund is automatically rebalanced on a regular basis.

Asset allocation therefore is a mechanism for balancing the elements of risk and reward and is one way of ensuring an element of diversification.

2.3 Volatile Markets

Conventional wisdom says investing in equities is more of a risk than bonds.

Well, if you are dipping in and out of the stock market trying to time your trades, you will almost certainly get caught out sooner or later so yes, more risky.

If you're paying over the odds in charges on your investments, your returns will suffer so yes - again more risky.

If you are hoping to make a quick profit on the markets over the next year or two, again you may be lucky but the chances are you will run a high risk of losing some of your investment.

Finally, you choose low cost investments, your money is being drip-fed into your investments on a regular basis - your plan is to invest for the long term… sounds good so far….suddenly, out of the blue, the stock markets turn negative, your investments lose 20% of their value overnight…panic, anxiety - what to do - sell now? Maybe hold on a while - sell when you get back to somewhere what you paid? Sell half now and keep your fingers crossed the remainder will turn out OK?

I believe this aspect is one of the key reasons why many private investors fail to achieve more success from their investing and this is why having some understanding of volatility of both the markets in general as well as the various asset classes is part of my ABC of investing.

When anxiety and fear suddenly enter the arena, its far more difficult to think rationally and make the right decisions. As a species we are not very well equipped to deal with uncertainty, so perhaps the answer is to approach investing from a position of absolute certainty - **markets will go up…**

and then go down. The other certainty is that no matter how far the markets fall, and then fall some more, **in the long run they always bounce back**.

Of course, we all like to know why things happen the way they do and we like to see patterns which may give us a clue as to how things will pan out in the future - its probably hard-wired into human DNA. All I've been able to work out is that markets are volatile - sometimes they go up and sometimes they are flat within a range and sometimes they fall. If you are investing on the stock market to secure a better return than cash deposits, **you need to accept this volatility as part of the deal**.

Volatility can be reduced by holding a higher proportion of less risky assets such as government bonds, corporate bonds and possibly property/commodities as a counterweight to equities. It is also usually a good idea to hold a geographically diverse portfolio (see later).

So, markets and share prices are volatile - for the day trader, this is where the action is, however as a total contrast, dividends are the sleepy backwater of the stockmarket, a positive oasis of calm. With most of the higher yielding shares and particularly investment trusts and index funds in my portfolio, the dividends are paid out on a regular quarterly of half yearly basis. The advantage of holding trusts is the dividend stream is more predictable and will increase a little each year to keep pace with inflation - more often than not, a little ahead. Even through the financial storm witnessed since 2008, most managed to maintain progressive payments.

Although an investor for many years, I am (still) learning to pay little or no attention to market 'noise', broker comments, media coverage and the ups and downs of the prices. More and more, my focus is mainly on the total return of my investments (part of which may include dividends) and their rate of increase - this is one of my personal strategies for coping with volatility.

Successful investing is all about the long term so it is vitally important to 'stay in the game' for many years. It is therefore important at the start of the process to find an investment balance and strategy that meshes well with your personality and temperament.

So, to return to the opening sentence, conventional wisdom says equities are more risky? Not in my book - yes there is no doubt they are more volatile than cash deposits - particularly individual shares - but you will need invest long term and possess the sort of mentality that can manage the inevitable up and down swings of the markets as part and parcel of the process.

I know equities give me a better return of income than cash deposits - they give me a better return than gilts and the rising dividends provide a hedge against inflation. However I also accept that holding a high proportion of equities would not be worth the additional anxiety so I find a mix with which I feel relaxed.

According to stockmarket legend Warren Buffett **"Risk comes from not knowing what you are doing"** - therefore, make sure you fully understand what you want to do and how you want to do it.

2.4 Diversify

My personal portfolio is split between investment trusts and index funds. I have been reducing my individual shares in recent times and replacing them with the more globally diverse index options - particularly the Vanguard Lifestrategy funds.

I hold several investment trusts - City of London and Temple Bar are a couple of my UK income selections, for a little exposure to smaller companies I chose Aberforth.

I usually update my portfolio holdings on a regular basis so reader can visit my blog for the current situation.

The point being, its not generally a good idea to put all your eggs in one basket. Pooled investment vehicles like investment trusts, exchange traded funds and OEICS, will typically hold one hundred or more individual shares and these are a simple way to diversify your portfolio. Indeed with the broadly diversified Vanguard LifeStrategy fund which is the latest addition to my portfolio, you have the option of a one-stop investment vehicle providing all the diversity and balance that may be required. Each fund in the LS range will hold over 1,000 individual securities (shares, bonds etc.)

Personally, I would never place all my investments with one fund or even several funds with just one provider. I like to spread the risk - some professionally managed investment trusts and some passive index funds.

However, some would argue it is possible to be over-diversified. According to modern portfolio theory, holding around 20 shares is around the optimum for adequate diversity and adding further shares has very little effect in reducing risk. Legendary investor Warren Buffett suggests that if you diversify too much you might not lose much but equally, you won't gain much either. His approach is to concentrate on companies he knows inside out and select a few well researched options out of which there is the expectation of some big 'winners'.

Buffett is exceptionally experienced, skilled and disciplined in his approach to investing - many try to emulate his success but no one has come close. A return of close to 20% compound annual growth over the past half century is a phenomenal achievement.

For the average small investor, I would think the better returns are more likely to be achieved from a **low cost, well diversified and balanced portfolio**. Whether to include individual shares or not is a matter of individual choice.

From my own experience, there is no doubt that the prices of individual investments can be very volatile at times - 2008/09 was a very good example - and this can provide opportune moments to acquire certain additions to the portfolio at a good yield (lower price).

2.5 Avoid High Charges

In his book **"Monkey with a Pin"** (free download from Amazon) Pete Comley suggests the average investor could be missing out on up to 6% in returns on their investments.

His research points to around 2% of this being attributed to charges.

Fundsmith manager Terry Smith says the average UK investor who invests via an adviser, uses a platform and then invests in mutual funds, incurs total charges of about 3 per cent each year.

Investment fund charges range between 1% and 2% - typically around 0.75% - 1.5% is the going rate for many depending on the class of fund selected. Traditionally, this figure has included a 0.5% trail commission which was paid to the platform or adviser however the introduction of RDR in 2013 has banned commission on new sales (but can remain for existing arrangements). However, these charges which appear in all the literature and comparison tables are **not the whole story**.

Although they are called 'total expense ratio' or now 'ongoing charges' - surprisingly, they do not include all the charges levied on the fund. For a start, they do not include transaction charges for the buying and selling of shares within the fund - nor do they include the 0.5% stamp duty on the purchases. The average 'churn' or portfolio turnover rate every year is around 50% - that means half of the shares held in the portfolio are likely to be traded in any given year. With some funds, the churn rate can be as high as 200% - which means the whole portfolio is turned over every 6 months. For every 10% of portfolio turnover, at least 0.2% is added in additional charges. This will typically add an extra 1% to the costs of holding the fund - more for less liquid markets like smaller companies and emerging markets funds.

Another 'hidden' fee that will impact on returns is soft commissions - fund managers deliberately hide costs that should properly fall under ongoing charges by inflating commissions on transactions.

The effect of these **'hidden extras'** will mean the average retail investor is paying not 1.0% or 1.5% in charges but possibly as high as 3%. That's 3% every year on the total value of your investments - whether they have performed well or not.

Over the years, there has been extensive studies and research that shows, over an extended period, most fund managers fail to consistently beat their benchmark. Research also shows that many small investors continue to waste money by paying active management fees for this consistent failure. This underperformance is not just due to poor asset allocation or stock selection, though this is a factor, but just as much the drag effect of the high charges affecting the fund performance. A bit like the boxer going into the ring with one hand tied behind his back - he'll land the odd lucky punch but 9 times out of 10 he's going to be knocked out.

As Anthony Hilton of the Evening Standard wrote a couple of years back – *"Remember, the only difference between investment professionals and investment amateurs is that the professionals make their mistakes with your money, not their own."*

For all the above reasons, with the **exception of low-cost index trackers**, I have tended to avoid funds or OEICs over the years and therefore tend to look at a mixture of low cost index funds and also investment trusts.

Lets take a brief look at the alternatives:

Low Cost Trackers As more people start to understand the drag effect of these higher charges on their investment performance, they are increasingly turning to low cost tracker funds. According to Investment Management Association figures, trackers accounted for around 11% of the private investor market in 2014.

Charges are typically in the region of 0.4% or less - the Vanguard FTSE UK Equity Index for example has a TER of just 0.08% (plus 0.5% stamp duty). Portfolio turnover rate is much lower on trackers - typically around the 10% - 15% range so the charges for this should be in the region of an additional 0.2%.

Alternatively, Vanguard offer a FTSE 100 ETF (exchange traded fund) with a TER of 0.1% plus the added advantage of no direct stamp duty on ETFs (but it will be paid for indirectly on the investments within the fund).

The difference between say 0.4% costs for a tracker and 2% - 2.5% real total costs on a managed fund will have a huge impact on returns. Lets take the example of a person with a £10,000 lump sum and investing £100 per month over 20 years - a total investment of £34,000. Assume a return of 6% p.a.

With the managed fund, after 20 years the investment would be worth **£50,828** and with the low cost tracker **£72,255** (comparison via Candid Money).

Investment Trusts I am an income investor and have used ITs for many years. A big reason for choosing trusts over funds was the typical lower charges - around 0.5% less - due to the fact they did not pay commission to intermediaries. With the introduction of Retail Distribution Review (RDR), the gap in charges has started to narrow.

TER can be as low as 0.4% on some trusts e.g. City of London and Bankers, but as with funds, there will be additional costs associated with transaction charges - portfolio turnover rate or 'churn' is usually lower with trusts - typically 20% to 30% on average.

I have not come across soft commissions with investment trusts - that's not to say it does not happen!

My best guess would be total charges between 0.4% and 1.2% - better than the average fund but not as good as low cost trackers. Whether fund managers can provide investors with added value for these extra charges is a huge subject which I do not intend to elaborate on here.

Individual Shares Potentially the cheapest way to invest for the long term buy-and-hold investor. The average cost on purchase via a low cost broker will be around £10 but can be as low as £1.50 via a regular investment option offered by some brokers - plus the usual 0.5% stamp duty.

That's it - no recurring annual fund/trust fees. For the long term buy-and-hold investor, this can be a very cost effective alternative. However you will need to hold a diverse range of shares - at least 20+ to be adequately diversified so the initial purchase costs and stamp duty will be a factor.

The other aspect to consider is volatility - too many unplanned sales and purchases will have an impact on overall costs.

2.6 Compound Returns

In my book **"DIY Pensions"**, I described the situation of two people, Alex and Sue. Sue started paying £2,000 per annum into her pension and continued for just 10 years. Alex started paying the same amount 10 years later than Sue and continued for 30 years. Sue paid in a total of £20,000 and Alex a total of £60,000. At retirement, Sue's pension pot was £100,000 more than Alex's!

The dramatic effects of this outperformance of Sue's fund are entirely due to the magic of compounding returns over a longer period - with a pension or investment, it will be the compounding of reinvested dividends - with cash savings, it is the effect of compounding interest on previous years interest.

So, whether you are investing for income via a stocks & shares isa or saving in a cash isa, the principle is the same - the sooner you can start, the more time your money will have to compound and grow.

There are basically just two elements to compound returns -

Time, and

Rate of Growth

Here's a simple example setting out the compound returns on savings of **£50 per month** over 10 years and 30 years. The rate of 2.5% roughly equates to current average building society or bank cash deposit rates and a figure of 9% is for long term returns on equities with dividends reinvested (allowing for minimal charges).

After 10 years, the cash deposit will provide a return of £6,812 whilst the equity return is £9,554. Over the longer period of 30 years, the cash deposit would return £26,696 whereas the equity fund with dividends reinvested would build up to an astonishing £85,717.

As you can see, the effect of compounding over the longer period year upon year on savings but particularly on the higher returning investments can make a huge difference to the final outcome. Equally, if you can save 1% or 2% on costs and charges in relation to investments, this will have a significant effect.

Albert Einstein described compound interest as "the greatest mathematical discovery of all time".

2.7 The Effect of Reinvesting Dividends

For most people reading this book, I imagine the aim will be to generate income for immediate use which is somewhat higher than returns on the average cash deposit account - if you are such a person this section will not apply.

However, investing for income can be used as a good long term strategy to build investments - whether in an ISA or pension/sipp and this method may even produce better returns than the traditional growth or mixed asset portfolio.

I suspect many people regard income investing as something to turn to when they are retired and in the earlier years, are better off going for growth investments. Indeed, this is exactly what I thought when I first started out on my investing journey in the late 1980s.

Looking at the whole spectrum of equities, some companies are priced more on a basis of their growth potential whilst others the share price will reflect more their income generating abilities. On average over the long term the equity market expects an annual total return across all equities of somewhere around 7%-8%. Its true that companies which do not pay out dividends to their shareholders can use more of their profits to reinvest in the business and this should lead to faster growth of the company and therefore its share price. The income investor will be looking more at companies which have the ability to provide more of the total return in the form of income as opposed to capital growth.

Research into the UK market carried out by **Dimson, Marsh and Staunton** of London Business School, covering the period 1900 - 2010 showed that a strategy of investing in higher yield shares produced a total return annualised at 10.9% whilst lower yielding shares produced a total return of just 8.0%.

The study also looked at the effect of reinvesting dividends and concluded the cumulative returns without reinvested dividends was 5.0% p.a. but were 9.4% including dividends reinvested.

Research carried out by **Morgan Stanley Global Equity Strategy Team** in 2012, came to a similar conclusion based on studies of the US markets since 1901. They found that compound annual growth rate for equities including dividends was 9.5% compared to 4.9% return excluding dividends. The researched pointed to dividends providing the majority of the investors total return during periods when markets were range bound or falling.

I hold **City of London Trust** in my income portfolio. If a lump sum of £35,000 was invested in the shares in 1983 and each years dividend reinvested in the purchase of further shares, the total investment pot would be worth over £1 million by the end of 2013.

Therefore, dividends are an important factor in achieving long term returns from investments. In fact, some might go as far as to suggest that investing via higher yielding investments could be the choice of long term growth investors as well as income investors.

One way to look at it is this, the average target return each year on my equity investments is in the region of 7% or 8% - so if I can secure a sustainable yield of 4% or 5%, I'm already more than halfway there.

2.8 Take Advantage of Tax Breaks

The vast majority of my investments are held in either my stocks & shares ISA or my flexi-access drawdown SIPP. There is no extra cost for holding my investments in an ISA, so even if there appears to be no immediate benefit, at the same time, there is no disadvantage.

ISA Whether you are saving in a building society deposit account or investing your money in the markets, it makes sense to take advantages of your annual ISA allowance. For 2017/18, every adult can save or invest up to £20,000 in their cash ISA or stocks & shares ISA and this will continue for 2018/19.

Prior to April 2016, 20% tax has been automatically deducted from interest on savings - basic rate tax payers would pay £20 tax on every £100 of interest on their savings. Now, interest on savings is paid gross i.e. without deduction of tax.

Introduced in April 2016, there is a new **Personal Savings Allowance** which introduces some big changes in the way savings are taxed. It is estimated that over 90% of savers will as a result pay no tax on their savings. Most savers will get up to £1,000 of interest on their cash savings tax-free.

Basic rate tax payers will therefore save up to £200 tax on their savings. The allowance for higher rate tax payers is £500 so they also will save up to £200 tax.

Previously it had been possible to transfer the value of a cash ISA into a stocks & shares ISA but not the other way. Now it is possible to transfer the whole or any part of an equities ISA to a cash ISA. Although in recent years, the returns offered by banks and building societies on cash deposits has been very poor, this will not continue for ever. As the economy recovers, interest rates will start to creep upwards and if inflation remains in low single figures, the rates on cash deposits may again become attractive. In such a situation, it will obviously be an advantage to have the option to transfer some gains built up in a stocks and shares ISA into a less volatile cash ISA.

One advantage of investing via an ISA is to avoid any possibility of becoming liable for **capital gains tax** (CGT). This would normally become due on a sale of investments which had risen in value by more than the annual CGT allowance - currently £11,300. Therefore for most people, this is unlikely to come into play but for those with more than, say £100,000 invested, a 10% rise in the stock market could easily trigger a potential CGT liability.

From 6th April 2016 the Dividend Tax Credit was replaced by a new **Dividend Allowance** of 0% tax on the first £5,000 of dividend income each year. (The chancellor has reduced this to £2,000 from April 2018)

Therefore you could have an income portfolio of £50,000 yielding 4% and not pay any tax. You could even have investments of £200,000 yielding 1% and still receive this income tax free.

Of course it would be sensible to take advantage tax breaks and hold investments in an ISA. Dividends received on shares held in an Individual Savings Account (ISA) will continue to be tax free. The limit for the coming tax year (2018/19) will continue at £20,000 for each person. A couple can therefore transfer £40,000 each year into a tax shelter.

Investors who receive over £2,000 dividend income (outside of their ISA) will pay tax of 7.5% for basic rate tax payers but a hefty 32.5% for higher rate tax payers. This is designed to deter owners of businesses who have gained an advantage in the past by taking income in the form of dividends rather than salary.

The big advantage for most people of holding investments in an ISA is there is no need to declare the income or gains on your annual tax return.

SIPP (Self Invested Personal Pension) I have included sipps mainly because of the significant changes to pensions. The main provision is, from **April 2015**, people with personal pensions have been free to access all of the money in their pension pot from age 55 years (but 57 yrs for younger people). The first 25% will be tax free however the remainder will only be taxed at marginal rates - for most people this will be 20% but for some it could be zero.

Whereas prior to these proposed changes, most retirees would only have the option of taking an annuity or possibly some form of capped/flexible drawdown, from 2015 retirees will have far more freedom and flexibility with options to take as much or as little as they require at any point in time. Personally, I have converted my SIPP to flexi-access drawdown rather than opt for taking an annuity. This means I have left the value of the pension pot invested - mainly in a range of investment trusts which provide a regular income. I regard it as a sort of index-linked annuity substitute.

Of course, as it is a pension, the sums withdrawn over and above the initial 25% will be taxable but unlike the ISA, there are tax advantages on all money paid into a pension subject to a cap of £40,000 per annum. For basic rate tax payers, for every £100 saved, the taxman will throw in a further £25 and for higher rate tax payers the top up from HMRC is £40.

I have covered this in more detail in "**DIY Pensions**" but believe with the new pension freedom and flexibility, SIPPs could become as popular as ISAs as a home for long term savings.

Lifetime ISA With the new Lifetime ISA, introduced from April 2017 anyone between the ages of 18 and 40 yrs can save as much or as little as they wish up to a maximum of £4,000 per annum. For savings up to the age of 50 yrs, the government will add a 25% bonus i.e a max. of £1,000 at the end of each year.

Therefore someone contributing the maximum from their 18th birthday could save £128,000 by the age of 50 yrs and receive total bonuses of £32,000.

The ISAs will operate similar to the existing system and individuals could have more than one Lifetime ISA - but only pay into one in any single year. They can choose between cash ISA or Stocks & Shares ISA

AIM Shares These are the shares issued by smaller companies listed on the Alternative Investment Market (AIM). These shares can now be held in an ISA and from April 2014, there is no longer the 0.5% stamp duty levied on purchase.

One of the attractions for wealthier investors of holding such shares is that after two years they become exempt for Inheritance Tax (IHT). This tax affects the estate of people with assets over £325,000 and is charged at 40%.

Other There are many other tax breaks available to the savvy investor which are beyond the remit of this book as I want to keep it fairly simple. I would suggest the following carry far more risk and are probably best avoided by the average small investor seeking income. For those adventurous souls who may want to do more research there are such things as Seed Enterprise Investment Scheme and Venture Capital Trusts (VCTs) to name but a couple.

2.9 DYOR - Do Your Own Research

This sounds fairly obvious but, from my viewing of various stock market related discussion boards, it is surprising how many people fail to adequately research the shares or investment trust/fund before they purchase. I suspect some would put more time and effort into researching their next holiday or smartphone purchase than an investment that could be providing an income for the next 20 or 30 years. Time spend on looking at some fundamentals will probably result in better returns over the longer term.

I will look at this in more detail later in the book but some time spent on research prior to purchase will almost certainly pay dividends (excuse the pun!) in the long run. How much research will, in some degree, depend on the time you have available and the approach you decide upon. For example, setting up a basic income-focussed passive tracker portfolio with 5 or 6 funds should be fairly straight forward and will therefore involve much less research than creating a portfolio with 20 individual shares and a basket of a further dozen or so investment trusts.

For those with little time for investing research and who may be just looking for a simple, no frills, low cost solution using passive index funds then they may like to check out my latest book 'DIY Simple Investing'.

2.10 An Investment Strategy Plan

If you were starting up a new business, one of the first things you would address would be the business plan. You would outline your aims and give a description of the product or service to be provided. You may look at your personal strengths and weaknesses and identify areas where you may need specialist expertise. You would look at projected income and expenditure and create a cash flow projection.

Writing a comprehensive business plan is, of course, no guarantee of success but it can go a long way in reducing the chances of failure.

The same principles hold true for investing. When you have taken some time to understand the investing process, it will be worthwhile to spend a little more time in creating a written strategy.

What level of income will be needed?

Estimated time frame?

Which Platform(s)?

What percentage allocated to equities?

Active or passive approach?

Which strategy offers the lowest costs?

Are you typically cautious or adventurous?

Percentage of equities/bonds/property in the mix?

Shares or investment trusts/funds/trackers/etf?

What percentage of cash to leave on bank/building society deposit?

Ways to cope with volatility and stay 'in the game'?

The main purpose of creating a plan is to clarify and record your thinking and strategy at the very start of the process and then you have a clear focus as you put the plan into action. By investing a little time on your plan before you start to invest your money, it should help to make your aims or goals appear more real.

Investing is a long-term project and there will be many dips and corrections in the markets - maybe a crash at some point. It is therefore important to have a good plan before setting out - *a plan which will help to keep you in the game over the longer term and particularly when the going gets volatile*.

There is no perfect strategy. Different plans will suit different investors with different circumstances. I suspect the best plan is one which is more likely to 'fit' with the individuals psychological make-up and is therefore most likely to keep them in the game and get them to their destination.

From time to time, as the plan unfolds and you gain more experience, it will be useful to review the plan and revise as necessary.

3. Different Types of Investments

In the UK, shares are bought and sold via the London Stock Exchange. The main market is the FTSE and this is sub-divided into the largest companies' shares called the FTSE 100, followed by the next tier of medium sized companies, FTSE 250 and then smaller companies found in the Small Cap index. Not all companies in the UK are listed on the stock exchange. Privately owned firms and co-operatives like John Lewis for example are not listed companies.

The principal reason for listing on the markets is to raise capital to expand the business. A company does this by issuing shares. Those shares are then bought and sold on the markets. The price of the shares will rise and fall according to supply and demand, news, trading results, market sentiment etc. Stock markets all around the world are intimately connected and tend to rise and fall together. The largest market is by far the New York Stock Exchange in the USA accounting for around 45% of world equities. The UK market, by comparison accounts for just 8%.

Some common ways to invest are :

Unit Trusts and OEICS

Investment Trusts (ITs),

Trackers & Exchange Traded Funds (or ETFs),

Direct Shares e.g. Vodafone, Tesco, BT etc.

Bonds & Fixed Interest

Lets take a look at these in a little more detail.

3.1 OEICs or Unit Trusts

These are a form of **'pooled investments'** run by a fund manager. The manager buys shares in a number of different companies and the investor buys 'units' in the fund. There are literally thousands to choose from - to get an idea of the different sorts, look at the likes of www.Trustnet.com.

Returns from the fund are paid through distributions. These can be monthly, quarterly or every six months, depending on the type of fund that you invest in. These distributions derive from the dividend payments received by the fund from the underlying shares within which they invest, or interest payments from bonds or even rental income in the case of property.

Most unit trusts and OEICs will give you two main options to choose from – income (inc) or accumulation (acc). Income units pay out the distributions as income, while accumulation units wrap up those distributions and reinvest them in the fund to increase the capital value of your investment. For those investors who need immediate income, obviously be sure to select the correct type of fund.

One drawback for income investors is that they are obliged to distribute all of the income (after charges) in the year it is received which means the dividend stream over time can be a little lumpy and unpredictable.

They are heavily promoted in the financial media and are popular with small private investors however, charges have tended to be a little on the high side for my liking, typically around 0.6% to 1.0% but up to 3% for more exotic sectors. A ban on payment of commission as part of the FCAs Retail Distribution Review resulted in lower charges which should bring their ongoing charges figure more into line with ITs.

There is now the up front platform charges of between 0.2% and 0.5% from your broker to compensate for the removal of commissions they previously received from the fund provider. When drawing up your strategy, it is important to be aware of all the known costs at the outset - so take account of fund charges **and** platform costs.

3.2 Investment Trusts

These are a little similar to unit trusts. They are a form of collective investment but ITs are a company in their own right. So, like shares in individual companies such as Unilever or BT, you buy and sell shares in the investment trust company - many of the larger trusts are listed on the FTSE 250 index. The actual share price at any given time may be less than the value of all the shares it holds and therefore the IT shares will trade at a discount to their net asset value (NAV).

As with any company quoted on the stock exchange, investment trusts have to publish an annual report and audited accounts. They also have a board of directors to which the manager of the trust is accountable and which looks out for the shareholder's interests. When you invest in an investment trust, you become a shareholder in that company. Should you have the time and inclination, you may attend the annual general meeting!

Investment Trusts have the advantage of being able to withhold some excess dividend income in good years and pay them out in poorer years, thereby smoothing the income payouts. As an income investor who holds several trusts, I find this aspect very beneficial as I can predict with a high degree of accuracy what income I can expect in future months and even years ahead. Some of the more consistent trusts e.g. City of London, have a record of paying steadily increasing dividends for over 50 years. This is one I have held in my portfolio for many years.

A major difference between investment and unit trusts is that investment trusts can borrow money to invest. This ability (known as **gearing**) can have a dramatic effect on the value of your investments.

Investment trusts use this borrowed money to invest in shares and other securities. Gearing is very useful when markets are rising as it magnifies any gains you make. However, when stock markets are falling, gearing will heighten your losses. A trust with a high level of gearing will therefore be more volatile under these circumstances than trusts with low gearing.

This means the more borrowing a trust has, the greater the risk to capital you face, but you also have the potential for higher returns. The combined effect of gearing and the discount means investment trusts are likely to be more volatile than the equivalent unit trust. This means if you invest in investment trusts you should expect a rockier road with bigger ups and downs.

Again there are many to choose from but, in the past they were not so heavily promoted as they did not offer commission to intermediaries. Charges since the introduction of RDR have come more into line with OEICs but I think, on average still tend to be a little lower, typically 0.75% or less, but can be higher for some sectors such as more globally focussed trusts and property ITs for example.

3.3 Tracker Index Funds and Exchange Traded Funds

One of the simplest ways to get started with investments is through an index tracker fund. These are low cost collective investment schemes that just follow the movement of an index. So when an index rises, the value of your fund rises with it (after costs). Conversely, when the index falls, your investment in the fund falls with it too. These are known as **passive investments**.

You can hold trackers in an OEICs or in an exchange traded fund (ETF) which are listed on the stock exchange like shares or investment trusts.

ETFs are a cheap way of tracking an index e.g. FTSE 100 or S&P 500 (United States). Unlike OEICs and ITs, they do not have a fund manager who will pick and choose which share to hold, rather they merely hold all the shares in a particular index. Charges are typically around 0.4% or less - some as low as 0.1% - so they can be a very cost effective way of investing.

Some ETF providers are, in no particular order, Vanguard, Blackrock iShares, ETF Securities (mainly commodities), State Street (SPDR range), HSBC, Lyxor and db x-trackers.

3.4 Active v Passive

Actively managed investment funds are, like their namesake, run by a professional fund manager or investment research team, who make all the investment decisions, like which companies to invest in or when to buy and sell different assets, on your behalf. They have extensive access to research in different markets, sectors and often meet with companies' senior management to analyse and assess their prospects before making a decision to invest.

The aim with active management is to deliver a return that is superior to the stock market that the companies sit within. An actively managed fund can offer you the potential for much higher returns than what a particular market is already providing.

Passive investing in tracker funds or ETFs will simply track a market, and charges will be far less in comparison. The funds are essentially run by computer and will buy all of the assets in a particular index, or the majority, to give you a return that reflects how the market is performing.

There are many supporters of the passive approach who point to its simplicity and low cost. Passive investing involves tracking an index, so if you decide to take that route, you need to decide which indices to track having regard to your asset allocation strategy. For the equity income seeker, a good index would be the FTSE 350 Higher Yield Index - only problem is, there is currently no passive investment on the market which tracks this index. The closest to it which I hold in my portfolio is the Vanguard FTSE UK Equity Income fund.

This is a fast moving and innovative industry so it may not be too long before new products appear to meet the increasing demand for a natural sustainable income. The nearest so far (see later) are the dividend aristocrats offered by SPDR.

3.5 Direct Shares

With ever increasing amounts of information available to everyone via the internet, it is relatively straight forward to research company profiles and their annual reports that, not so long ago, would only be available to a stockbroker. Also, with the increasing popularity and low cost of online brokers, it has never been easier to put together your own portfolio of shares.

Shares in blue chip FTSE 100 companies are most widely held by individual private investors - Marks & Spencer, Shell Oil, Vodafone, BT and National Grid are well known and commonly held shares.

The cost of purchase is typically around £10 - £12 but can be as little as £1.50 (plus 0.5% stamp duty) via a low cost execution-only broker, so for a long term 'buy and hold' investor it can be an extremely economical method to invest for income. There should be no more ongoing costs so, over the longer term, this could work out more economical than Unit Trusts or Investment Trusts.

The main drawback I find in holding individual shares is their **volatility**. Share prices can swing up and down by 10% or 20% in a matter of days. No matter how relaxed you are about volatility, it can be very disconcerting to buy a carefully researched share and find it is worth 25% less than you paid for it some 6 months earlier and the dividend reduced or suspended. Secondly, if the company runs into problems, it is not uncommon for the board to reduce or even suspend the dividend payments. Should this occur to one or two shares in you 20 share portfolio, your income could drop by 10%.

It will, therefore be important to ensure you are the sort of person who can manage the emotional rollercoaster which will be an inevitable part of holding shares and also to hold a diverse portfolio of shares, say at least 20 to help minimise risk.

Many small private investors may hold a mixed variety of investments - shares, investment trusts, OEICs and/or index trackers in their portfolios.

3.6 Bonds & Fixed Interest

Depending on your allocation decision between the balance of equities to bonds, it is likely that most investors will want some element of fixed income in the mix. My personal preference is for 40% of my total income portfolio allocated to a diverse mixture of government bonds, corporate bonds and fixed interest securities. Younger people with a longer timeframe may well decide on a higher percentage of equities.

The mix could include such securities as retail bonds and preference shares. You could look at higher yielding corporate bonds via investment trusts or ETF providers like iShares. To assist with balance and smooth out the volatility of equities, it will also be appropriate to look at government bonds and inflation linked gilts.

With a combination of well chosen fixed interest securities, it should be possible to obtain a solid natural yield in the region of 3% - 4% or thereabouts without too much difficulty.

The interest on gilts, corporate bonds and PIBS is paid gross and if they are held within an ISA (or SIPP) there is no tax to pay.

The advantage of a proportion of the portfolio being held in fixed interest is firstly the generally higher yield over equities and also that future income payments are likely to be a known quantity, unlike dividends from equities, which may be held flat or reduced in times of low profitability.

This makes bonds ideal for people who wish to secure future income over a defined period of time. They add a degree of solidity and certainty to the income stream as well as reducing volatility of the capital value of the total portfolio.

4. Sustainable Income

We have looked at a few of the basics of investing and also the various ways to invest. I will therefore cover some of the particular areas I focus upon when investing for income from my capital.

For me, investing is about not just income but the level of total return on my investments, but more than this, its about a **sustainable return,** investments which can deliver a growing stream of income and growth far into the future which will keep pace with and hopefully exceed inflation.

I am not looking to make a quick killing by selling when the share price has risen - this is a long term buy-and-hold strategy.

4.1 Dividend Yield

The yield on a share is fairly simple to work out. It is merely the **annual dividend per share divided by the current share price**. You will sometimes see the expression <u>historical yield </u>which uses the last full years dividend actually declared and paid in the above calculation, even though you may be well into the next years trading cycle.

When I am looking at my income projections for the coming year, I may well try to assess <u>forward yield </u>on my portfolio. Based on the rate of dividend growth in recent years, I will factor in the anticipated rise for the coming financial year for any particular share and compare this to analysts estimates on e.g. Digital Look - this is forward yield. The same can be done with investment trusts which mostly try to gradually increase dividend payouts year-on-year.

When calculating yield, do not rely upon the data provided by your screening website - it could be out of date or just plain wrong! Always check the official results from a company's own website or via announcements on the likes of Investegate etc.

4.2 Higher Yielding Shares

As I have pointed out earlier, the FTSE 100 accounts for around 90% of all dividends paid so this is the obvious starting point in your search for dividends. It is of course possible to merely purchase a FTSE 100 low cost tracker and sidestep all the research involved in setting up a shares portfolio - this should deliver the average yield on all 100 FTSE constituents - currently around 3.5% per annum.

The drawback with this approach is that you are holding all 100 shares in the FTSE 100 index but most of the income is derived from around 50% of the companies in the index. For a start, not all of the companies pay dividends, others focus more on growth and pay only a modest 1% or 2% dividend, some have encountered difficulties in recent years and have cut their dividend others carry what I would consider to be unacceptably high levels of debt etc. etc.

Another collective solution would be the Vanguard Equity Income fund mentioned above. This will give investors access to a broad range of dividend-paying securities from across the (mainly) FTSE 350, while reducing the risk of being overly invested in a small number of high-paying shares or particular industry sectors by limiting the percentage of the index invested in any one company or industry.

I imagine many income investors may prefer to select their own portfolio of shares and in so doing, they can focus on what they perceive to be **quality companies** which pay a reasonable dividend, which has risen steadily over at least the past 5 years (preferably longer) and which they believe are very likely to continue to do for many years to come.

4.3 Defensive Shares

Large defensive stocks can offer relatively low risk exposure to the long term compound growth of stock markets. They contrast with what are known as cyclical shares which tend to rise and fall with the fortunes of the economic cycle - a good example would be house builders or mining companies.

The investor attracted to such investments will hold a portfolio which is weighted more towards these solid defensives and whose sales and business performance are not so highly correlated with the overall economic cycle. These companies tend to be focussed on such sectors as food, beverages, pharma, tobacco and utilities. Whatever is happening to the economy, we all need food and drink; we all get sick or old and need healthcare; we all use gas, electricity and telecoms etc.

In the USA, the best performing stocks over the past 20 years are all defensives - the likes of Marlboro maker Altria Tobacco, Coca-Cola, Pepsi, Kraft-Heinz, pharma company Pfizer and Proctor & Gamble - makers of Ariel, Gillette and Pampers.

Which brings me on to the next sub heading….

4.4 Economic Moats

One particular aspect I look out for as a sign of quality is some form of competitive advantage - this could be in the form of a worldwide patent on a new product or more commonly, an attractive brand which can maintain strong consumer loyalty and be rolled out globally. A company that's afraid of competition is going to be less likely to increase its dividend as quickly as a company that feels very comfortable about its business.

Warren Buffett coined the term 'economic moat' to describe a business' competitive advantage that keeps other companies at a disadvantage. He said : "The key to investing is not assessing how much an industry is going to affect society, or how much it will grow, but rather determining the competitive advantage of any given company and, above all, the durability of that advantage. The products or services that have wide, sustainable moats around them are the ones that deliver rewards to investors".

One area that the small private investor does not often focus on is **brands**. Those companies with strong brands have a significant competitive advantage which will, over time, translate into outperformance and result in increasing shareholder returns.

Strong brands enable their companies to charge premium prices for their goods; not just because customers already know what they're getting but also because humans are instinctively cautious about things that they've never tried before - we tend to be creatures of habit.

According to a study done by Credit Suisse, companies that focus on brand building by spending at least 2% of sales on marketing outperformed the S&P 500 by more than 4% annually since 1997. The top 20% of the companies featured in the research outperformed the market by 17% annually over the same period.

Some well known brand names from large companies listed on the UK stock market include: Flora margarine, Johnnie Walker whiskey, Sure Deodorant, Cillit Bang, PG Tips, Dettol, Gaviscon, Durex, Guinness and Magnum ice cream. These names would probably be recognised all around the world.

4.5 Payout Ratio

If a company is paying out nearly all of its earnings in dividends, this may be a sign that the dividend is not sustainable. Furthermore, if the payout ratio is increasing over time, this might indicate that earnings growth is not keeping up with dividend growth, and the dividend is not sustainable.

In the search for quality companies with a sustainable dividend, check to see what proportion of annual earnings are paid out to the investor in dividends and what proportion is left to be reinvested in the business. I try to look for a pay-out ratio of between 40% - 60%. Higher than average yield is a significant factor but a lower pay-out ratio is usually a positive sign. Payout ratio is the inverse of dividend cover (see later) - if the cover is 2x the payout ratio will be ½ i.e. 50%.

4.6 Dividends Signal a Well-Run Company

Unlike some of the figures presented in a company's results such as earnings, the physical payment of a dividend cannot be distorted or manipulated. Therefore a record of gradually increasing dividend payouts stretching back over many years is, for me, evidence that the management is running a well disciplined ship. Dividends are the strongest signal of capital discipline, and the measure that most clearly and objectively reveals the underlying health and strength of a business.

It is not difficult to check the dividend history of any particular share or investment trust. The best place to start is the company's own website - alternatively, it will be available via the 'fundamentals' information on such research sites as Digital Look for example.

4.7 Taxation of Savings Interest & Dividends

From April 2016, interest from savings is no longer taxed at source. There is now a personal savings allowance and everyone can receive up to £1,000 tax free interest for basic rate taxpayers (£500 for higher rate taxpayers) on their cash savings and in addition, they can also receive up to £5,000 tax free on any dividends from investments.

5. Set Up Your Portfolio

So we have covered the basics of investing and have worked out a sensible plan setting out aims and objectives, a time scale and a plan of action. Its time to look at the practical side of setting up a portfolio and one of the first thing is to choose your online broker(s).

5.1 Selecting Your Online Broker

As I said in my introduction, investors now have much greater options on how and where to invest than ever before. The low cost, online execution-only broker is the perfect platform for the diy investor.

I have held all my investments with such brokers since 2001 and find it is so much easier than the old system of holding share certificates.

With online brokers, your investments are held in a nominee account which means you will not receive a share certificate so there is no 'paperwork' to attend to. The online execution-only broker is not legally permitted to offer advice to its customers.

Lets take a look at some of the factors to take into account when selecting an online broker.

* Does the broker offer the type of investment you wish to hold in your portfolio? Seems fairly obvious but some brokers may not offer a full range of low cost trackers - others may offer only a limited range of investment trusts etc.

* Charges - what is the platform fee? Some brokers are more competitive for funds - others for shares, investment trusts and ETFs. Some offer to cap charges above a certain portfolio value.

* Are you happy with the platform interface - is it intuitive and therefore easy to find your way around?

* What range of analysis tools are offered? It can be an advantage to view your portfolio online and also to maintain a 'watchlist portfolio' of investments you may wish to follow and analyse for the future. You may wish to filter shares or investment trusts for things like size, dividend yield, cover etc.

* If you will be drip-feeding your money into the investments over a prolonged period, it will make sense to choose a broker who does not charge a dealing fee for funds or can offer a low cost regular investment option.

* If you are likely to hold shares and/or investment trusts, check the situation regarding re-investing of dividends - is there a facility for this to be done automatically and if so, is there a charge?

*Check if there are additional charges for telephone trades. With my online broker AJ Bell YouInvest, its an extra £20 for telephone trades and some investments cannot be traded online.

* Check the level of exit fees in the event you wish to move to another broker. Typical fees are usually based on whether you wish to transfer your portfolio over without having to sell and then repurchase with the new broker and will be

around £20 - £30 per line of stock. Obviously, if you hold many different investments, it could be very expensive to transfer out.

* Is it likely you will want to hold overseas listed investments? If so, make sure this option is available and check out any additional costs.

* Finally, having narrowed down the list of candidates, you may want to give the broker a call to confirm everything is still in accordance with your research and also see how their customer services respond to your questions.

5.2 Comparison Sites

Investment providers broadly fall into two groups – those that charge a **percentage fee** which are obviously good if you have smaller amounts invested - probably the norm for most investors in the early years, and those that charge a **flat fee** which is possibly the better choice for larger sums.

Some brokers will be better for those with funds whilst others may suit those who prefer shares, investment trusts or ETFs as they offer to cap fees above a certain amount.

If you will be drip-feeding your money into the investments over a prolonged period, it will make sense to choose a broker who can offer low cost options. Some brokers make no transaction charge for the purchase of funds. Many offer a regular investment discount - maybe £1.50 or £2.00 for the regular purchase of investments.

For those diy investors who are seeking a passive approach to running a portfolio using mainly index funds and ETFs, Monevator provides a regularly updated comparison table covering most of the popular discount brokers and fund platforms. Also comparefundplatforms.com - provides an interactive process.

There is probably no single best broker, the best one for any individual will be the one that ticks the most boxes according to that individuals specific situation and requirements.

Of course, you may wish to have more than one broker. Personally, I use AJ Bell Youinvest for my investment trusts (mainly) and then Halifax Share Dealing for my Index Funds as the annual charges are a flat-fee of £12.50 per year.

I have listed some of the more popular brokers at the end of this book.

5.3 Selecting Your Investments

As you will have given some thought already to your strategy whilst preparing your plan and selected a suitable broker, the next stage is to select the appropriate investments

The concept of investing for income is possibly as old as the stock market itself and many column inches have been written in the financial press describing the different approaches.

When I started my blog site in 2013, I was using a combination of individual shares (35%) and investment trusts (65%) which worked just fine for several years. However,

5A Individual Shares

5A.1 Narrow Down the Options

According Capita Dividend Monitor, total dividends paid by all companies on the UK market in 2000 were £42 bn and by 2017 this had grown to £90 billion. Over half of the total dividends paid were provided by the top 15 companies and the FTSE 100 accounts for around 90% of dividends so, in my book, this is the obvious place to begin the trawl.

Spend a little time to research the FTSE 100 - I use the Interactive Investor 'stock filter' tool (News & Research tab) - as they were my former online broker before I moved my account to AJ Bells YouInvest. You could equally use Digital Look and many other research sites.

In 'Basic Settings' select 'FTSE 100' from the dropdown Index box - from the 'advanced settings' you could use dividend yield and dividend cover min/max values to help narrow down the selection. By then clicking the **'Display Results'** box at the end, you will be presented with a list of shares from the FTSE 100 which meet the criteria you have chosen.

From this list, it should be possible to draw up a shortlist of say, 25 of the highest yielding shares. I am looking for what I regard as quality companies which I hope can deliver a long-term sustainable income.

Tempting though the higher yield may be, the next step is to discard ones whose yield is too high - if the yield is more than double the average for the FTSE 100 the market may be indicating problems down the road so, although tempting, these shares are best avoided. Personally, I would be looking at an overall initial target yield of around 1.0% above the FTSE 100 average. At the time of writing the FTSE is yielding 3.7% so maybe looking in the region of 4.0% - 4.5%.

As this is a long term project - I suggest a minimum of 10 years - you are looking for companies that can deliver a **sustainable and growing dividend** year after year. From your shortlist, you will need to identify which companies have delivered a growing dividend for at least the past 5 years. You can do this by looking up each company on the Interactive Investor site and navigating to the fundamentals page which shows the dividend payment at the foot of the page.

5A.2 Dividend Cover

Dividend cover is an indicator of how safe the dividend payout is going to be in the future. The way to work out cover is to simply divide the earnings per share (EPS) by the full year dividend per share. So, for example if EPS is 50p and dividend is 25p the cover will be 2x.

The dividends should be well covered by earnings - I suggest a minimum of 1.5 times, but preferably 2x or above. Again you can use the stock filter tool to remove companies with dividend cover of say, less than 1.5x.

5A.3 Free Cashflow Cover

One of the aspects I look for in a company's fundamentals is the ratio of cash from operations less capital expenditure. Free cash flow is how much cash flow is left over each year after the company has reinvested in its business. Think of it as spare or surplus cash flow. It's from these surplus cash flows that dividends, buybacks, debt repayments, etc. are funded. The degree of cover can be thought of as your dividend "margin of safety".

This figure is fairly easy to work out. From the annual accounts, navigate to the "Cash Flow Statement". Find the figure for **Cash from Operations** then deduct the figure for **Capital Expenditure** (this may be referred to as 'Additions to Property, Plant & Equipment') then divide by total dividends paid for the year to give a figure for FCF cover. I like a ratio over 1.0x and preferably over 2.0x. The higher the ratio, the more secure I feel that the company can maintain a growing dividend.

5A.4 Diverse Selection

You do not want all your selections in the same category. There may be some sectors you wish to avoid entirely - some people object on ethical grounds to such sectors as tobacco, alcohol or companies manufacturing arms etc.

All shares are categorised by the sort of business they undertake e.g. transport, supermarkets, oil producers, household goods, general retail, financials such as banks etc. Again, these can be researched on the Interactive website under 'Tools & Research' tab.

The next step is to narrow down your list to just one or at most two from each sector of the market. It is important to have a diverse portfolio of individual shares - I suggest at least 20 - as there will inevitably be one or two disappointments down the line.

For example, Shell and BP are both FTSE 100 companies from the same sector - oil producers - and offer a similar yield. Do you want to hold shares in this sector? If so, do you prefer one over the other or do you hold both. Likewise with tobacco companies in the same sector are Br. American Tobacco and Imperial Brands.

As you are preparing your shortlist of possible candidates, there will be several areas where a similar choice will be offered. Other examples would be supermarkets Tesco/Sainsbury, pharma companies GlaxoSmithKline/AstraZeneca, miners Rio Tinto/BHP Billiton.

Some investors like a focussed portfolio - around 20 shares and to select just one from any sector. If you decided to hold a 30+ share portfolio, it could be an advantage to choose a couple from some sectors according to personal preference.

5A.5 Debt and Gearing

Try to ensure your selections do not have too much debt on their books - sometimes called 'gearing'. Some borrowing can help a company to grow and the additional profits from that growth pay off the borrowing - a little like borrowing on mortgage to buy a house. However, if there is a downturn in the companies business or if interest rates rise quickly, profits may come under pressure and more money is needed to repay debt which leaves less for dividends.

All too often companies overextend themselves and end up either cutting the dividend or cancel it altogether, which is obviously not good for income seeking shareholders. We saw what happened to bank shares in 2008!

When I was looking for possible candidates for my portfolio, I look for those preferably with no debt but draw the line at a maximum of 50% net gearing.

I used **Digital Look** (registration required but free!) to research the gearing for any company I was interested in. Look up the company in the search box, then navigate to 'financials' then 'fundamentals' and the net gearing figure should be at the bottom.

5A.6 Foreign Exchange

The FTSE 100 is made up of large global companies. In the energy and mining sector, all the companies operate in a market where the commodities are denominated and traded in US dollars. They are together responsible for around a quarter of all dividends paid.

Just two banking companies, HSBC and Standard Chartered are responsible for 10% of dividends paid - both do much of their business outside of the UK and report in USD.

The rate of exchange between the US dollar and GB pound will have some impact on the amount of dividends received after conversion. In the period to April 2014, the pound strengthened considerably rising from $1.49 to $1.68 which means UK income investors received less dividends in sterling terms than the previous year. However, post Brexit, we saw sterling fall dramatically against both the USD and Euro.

Currency movements can work for or against you and are difficult to predict. (Some fund managers try to reduce or avoid this risk by 'hedging' currency exposure. This means they take out a form of insurance to protect against currency movements, for better or worse).

5A.7 The Shortlist

Having worked through the above steps, you should now have a shortlist of FTSE 100 higher yield shares which are from diverse sectors of the market, a good track record of payments in previous years, low(ish) borrowing, adequate cash flow cover and well covered dividend yield.

If you aim for a portfolio of 20 holdings, then you can set limits for the weight of each holding relative to the average holding weight. In such a situation, you could decide to allocate a larger percentage of your investment to the larger companies or FTSE 'heavyweights' or you could allocate 5% of your starting capital to each company. This is important, because the market will rise and fall, and each of your holdings take on a life of their own.

To see if you are on track with your initial selection of shares, have a look at the top holdings of a couple of Investment Trusts in the UK Income sector on e.g. Trustnet.

I hold City of London Trust in my income portfolio and at the time of writing, their top ten (from a total of 120) holdings are:- Shell Oil (5.8%), HSBC (4.7%), Br. American Tobacco (4.5%), Diageo (3.2%), BP (3.0%), Vodafone (2.7%), Prudential (2.7%), Unilever (2.6%), Lloyds Bank (2.6%) and RELX (2.4%).

You should be able to get a sufficiently diverse portfolio from FTSE 100 shares, but if you are struggling then look at shares in the upper reaches of the FTSE 250.

To summarise, a strategy focussed on picking solid shares with a reasonable yield, hold a reasonably diversified portfolio, and avoid 'yield traps' and over-trading should deliver the desired results for the patient investor with the ability to cope with volatility.

With careful share selection and good diversification, the income should increase by at least the rate of inflation over the long term. A growing income will, over time, be rewarded by capital growth provided that the shares were initially bought at a reasonable price, which is likely to be the case if the initial yield was already above average.

Capital value is determined by the rise and fall of the individual share prices and is much more volatile than the year on year steady rise in dividends. It may take some time to adjust psychologically but the capital value of the portfolio should be ignored to a large extent (personally I find this difficult!).

For those investors who find they cannot deal with this volatility, or feel the selection process is too complex or just do not have the time to do the research, the solution will be to avoid individual shares and opt for some form of collective route.

I started my personal finance blog in February 2013 and regularly post articles relating to the investments I hold so anyone is free to check out the latest portfolio update at www.diyinvestoruk.blogspot.co.uk

My individual shares portfolio has been gradually wound down following a review of strategy in 2015 and the final remaining shares were sold in 2017.

5.B Investment Trusts

5B.1 Narrow Down the Options

As with shares, first of all spend a little time to draw up a list of possible candidates for your portfolio. A good place to begin this research is the Association of Investment Companies - www.theaic.co.uk

There are currently over 400 trusts which cover many different sectors and styles. The number of different trusts to hold in a portfolio will vary according to degree of diversity, areas to invest in etc - are you using ITs for all your income generation or does it form a smaller part of a larger portfolio?

Personally, I now use a mix of trusts and index funds for my equity portfolio and a smaller part of my fixed income portfolio and therefore would be looking for around a dozen or so in total - possibly 3 or 4 from the UK Income sector, a couple more from the Global Income sector, maybe Commercial Property, possibly a smaller companies trust and so forth so that you end up with a diverse selection of income producing ITs. Other possibilities would be infrastructure - including renewable energy.

If you select the tab 'Find & Compare Investment Companies' then from the 'Investment Needs' box select 'Income' the page will load all companies in alphabetical order.

If you then click on the "total assets" column (left of page) this will arrange the list in order of size - largest at the top. I tend to make my selection from trusts with a market cap. above £250m. so this would narrow down the possible candidates to around 10 from this sector.

Alternatively select 'UK Equity Income' or 'Global Eq Income' and again, filter by size to eliminate the smaller players.

Next, select the "Dividend yield" tab and again click the end column to sort by portfolio yield. On the same page, have a look at 5yr dividend growth.

The next column to look at is "Ongoing Charges/gearing" and sort by ongoing charges plus performance fee. Obviously the trusts with the lower charges and possibly no performance fee would be the favourites to investigate further.

It is always worthwhile checking the total return for each trust over various periods - sometimes a trust has a modest yield but a very good overall return. I would place a couple of my holdings, Finsbury Growth & Income managed by Nick Train and Scottish Mortgage Trust in this category.

The sectors which traditionally provide a higher natural yield would be Infrastructure & Renewable Energy, UK Equity & Bond Income, Private Equity, Property, UK Income and Global Equity Income.

It should not be too difficult to select a shortlist of maybe 10 - 15 trusts. If you click on each individual trust title, you will be directed to a separate dedicated page from where you can continue your research, check out current fact sheet, view the latest annual/half-year reports and also add to your AIC watch list if required.

The aim will be to select trusts which have a good long-term track record relative to their benchmark and ideally, a trust manager who has been in the post for some years. For example, Job Curtis at City of London has been manager since 1991.

Each investment trust will publish its annual report each year and these are freely available to everyone and anyone who may be interested. It is usually worthwhile looking up the reports for the past year for each of your short listed selections. Make sure the trust has the objectives of increasing dividends for shareholders, maybe couched in terms of 'real growth' which merely means faster than inflation.

5B.2 Discount to NAV (Net Asset Value)

Investment trusts are quoted on the stock market like any other share and their price fluctuates mainly as a result of basic supply and demand. When demand is high prices rise to, or above, NAV. When demand is low, they can slump to prices below NAV.

If a trust is trading at a 5% discount to NAV, for every 95p you spend, you receive £1 of assets. Conversely, if a trust is trading at a premium of 10%, the underlying shares in the trust are valued at less than the price you are asked to pay for the shares in the trust. A trust can, and often does trade at either a premium or discount to NAV for many months or even years.

As far as I am concerned, although it is naturally an advantage to purchase at a discount, if all other criteria is satisfactory and meets my quality assurance checks and the yield is what I require, I will be prepared to purchase not withstanding any premium. Some investors will never purchase at a premium - each to their own particular strategy.

5B.3 Revenue Reserves

Investment trusts can retain part of their dividend income each year and transfer this to their revenue reserve. The revenue reserve has a key role to play when it comes to maintaining a regular flow of dividend payments - the reserve can be built up in good years and tapped into in lean years.

For the income investor, it is reassuring to know your investment has accumulated the equivalent of the next 18 months or 2 years dividend in its reserves.

5B.4 Diversity

The advantages of holding ITs and other collectives is that each one will hold many different shares selected by the trust manager, typically between 40 and 100 so, whereas you will need to hold 20 individual shares for a modestly diversified share portfolio, you only need a couple of ITs to achieve the same objective. Also, a good manager will be constantly keeping all the constituents of the trust under review and will dispose of weaker shares and replace with better prospects. For this professional management, you will pay an annual fee of between 0.4% - 1.0% which, over time, will have an impact on overall returns.

5B.5 Trusts or Shares?

For me, and I am sure many other small investors, the objective is to obtain a reasonable level of sustainable income which will rise in line with inflation, or a little ahead whist at the same time preserving and/or increasing the original capital.

I have been running a my natural income portfolio of investment trusts for the past 9 years and monitor the progress of each at the end of each year. This time frame is now a reasonable length and I found the returns from my basket of income trusts were always slightly ahead of my individual shares portfolio - maybe an average of just 1% or 2% each year on a total return basis (capital & income combined). My shares portfolio turned out to be the weakest link in my strategy which was another reason to change tack.

This may not seem much, but as we have seen in an earlier chapter, small amounts compounded over many years can have a significant impact.

There are probably a number of factors - the effect of gearing during a generally rising market (2010 - 2017) will certainly have had a beneficial effect boosting the returns for the trusts, also the use of options to generate greater income will also be a factor as well as the professional skill of the manager and his/her team in stock selection and asset allocation. Then again, it could well be I was not very good at selecting shares!

For those investors who choose not to hold individual shares, they may very well find get as good or even better returns from just holding a diverse selection of investment trusts and index funds or even a simple selection from the multi-asset option. Its really a choice for each individual to decide.

Some trusts are held in my ISA, some in my SIPP drawdown portfolio (and some in both)

5.C Bonds & Fixed Interest Securities

The last forty or fifty years have seen the emergence, growth and eventually the almost total domination of the "cult of the equity". Prior to this, pension funds had invested mainly in bonds, the view being that fixed income securities were a logical and safe home for the money.

All this changed in the 1950's, in a move largely credited to the then fund manager of Imperial Tobacco, George Ross Goobey who reached the conclusion that equities were undervalued and started switching the fund into the then unfashionable stock market.

With an ageing population in most developed countries, income becomes an increasingly valuable aspect for any portfolio. Income available from some bonds and other fixed interest securities is generally higher than that available from equities. Also, future income payments should be a known quantity, unlike dividends from equities, which may be reduced or withheld entirely in times of low profitability.

Therefore fixed income should be a consideration for investors who wish to secure future income over a defined period of time.

5C.1 Yield

Yield is the rate of return generated by an investment in a particular bond. The following types of yield calculations may be used

Flat Yield This calculation takes into account only the return generated by the coupon and does not factor in any capital gain or loss on the bond throughout its lifetime. Flat yield therefore expresses the return generated only by the interest paid on the bond and not by any profit or loss that the bondholder may incur by holding the bond until its maturity. Flat yield = (annual coupon / price) x 100

The **Gross Redemption Yield** calculation offers a more complete measure of yield than that provided by the flat yield as it takes both coupon payments and capital gain or loss into account. It involves a more complex calculation based on the present value cash flows of the bond. The Gross Redemption

Yield reflects the 'internal rate of return' of the bond, i.e., the discount rate that, when applied to the future cash flows of the bond produces the current price of the bond.

With bonds & FI paying semi-annually, quarterly or sometimes monthly, a carefully chosen portfolio with several diverse holding can produce a reliable monthly income. As mentioned earlier, most bonds pay their coupons gross, without withholding tax. Investors can take advantage of this by holding qualifying bonds within an ISA (or sipp), thereby producing a tax free income.

5C.2 Narrow Down the Options
The first port of call (for me) for researching this area is via **Trustnet** (www.trustnet.com). From the "investments" tab, select "Unit Trusts & OEICs" then "prices & performance" - from the fund focus dropdown box select "Fixed Interest" and click go - this should present around 300 or so funds.

These can then be filtered according to Risk Score. Click this heading and the funds will be arranged in order with lowest, around 10 at the top and the highest risk funds at the bottom of the list.

FE Risk Scores provide a single, simple measure of risk across a broad range of investments. In the UK FE Risk Scores measure the riskiness of instruments relative to the FTSE100. Weekly volatility is measured over three years with recent behaviour counting more heavily than earlier behaviour. FE Risk Scores are calculated weekly, and can be tracked over time.

Cash type investments will have scores close to zero, mutual funds will tend to have scores in the 0-150 range, while equities will generally be in excess of 100.

Generally speaking, the lower the risk score, the lower the yield.

A further option available on the Trustnet site is via the "Tools" tab and filter by e.g. "Crown Fund Rating" and your chosen band for risk scores. FE Crown Fund Ratings enable investors to distinguish between funds that are strongly outperforming their benchmark and those that are not.

The top 10% of funds will be awarded five FE Crowns, the next 15% receiving four Crowns and each of the remaining three quartiles will be given three, two and one Crown respectively.

Although I have tended to avoid OEICs for equities, the charges for some of the so called 'clean class' of FI fund are reasonably competitive on costs - a common figure is around 0.75% - so they could well be worth a look for those preferring a managed approach.

Having narrowed down the list, it will then be a case of clicking on each fund from your chosen selection to check out more detail such as current yield, investment objectives, ongoing charges figure (ignore annual management charge or AMC) and sector weightings etc. As with investment trusts, it will always be worthwhile downloading the latest managers report as well as the current fact sheet.

Another source for research is **Fixed Income Investments** (www.fixedincomeinvestments.org.uk) which is a free resource for those wishing to research bonds, PIBS, preference shares as well as an indication of the possible yield at any particular point in time.

As an example, select the "FI Prices" tab and from the dropdown menu, choose PIBS (permanent interest bearing shares issued by building societies). A table of all available PIBS will appear and from this it will be possible to narrow down options according to required yield, call date, current spread etc.

The process will be the same with other sectors - preference shares (non financial), insurance bonds etc.

Another possibility is a collective approach via investment trusts. As before, using the **AIC website**, select "UK Equity & Bond" sector and filter according size, yield, share price return over the past 5 years etc.

Unfortunately, I find at the present time, ITs do not have a marvellous selection to choose from - the only ones I hold currently are CQS New City High Yield (NCYF) and City Merchants HY Trust.

5C.3 PIBS

In recent years, a popular fixed income assets held by private investors in the UK were PIBS - Permanent Interest Bearing Securities. These subordinated instruments were originally issued by many of the well-known building societies who, unable to raise equity finance in the same way as banks, used the PIBS structure to bolster their balance sheet.

The safety of capital and income from these investments was questioned during the credit crunch of 2008/09 when the likes of Northern Rock and Bradford & Bingley got into severe difficulties and some investors lost money.

Since that time, many of the stronger societies have survived the financial turmoil and strengthened their balance sheets.

Most PIBS can be redeemed or "called" at the issuer's option on certain dates, or the issuer may have the right to reset the coupon from a fixed payout to something tied to base, LIBOR or gilt rates. In the past, almost all calls were exercised. But with interest rates now so low, issuers are increasingly faced with incredibly tempting coupon reset rates which could slash their cost of capital. This reset rate is therefore something to pay particular attention to if considering PIBS for part of your portfolio.

I had holdings with Coventry BS and Nationwide BS which I purchased at a very attractive price following the turmoil of 2008/09. They were both redeemed in 2016. The double digit yields offered in 2009 - 2011 are no longer available, however I believe PIBS with some of the stronger/larger building societies may still be worthy of consideration for income seekers - maybe as a small proportion of a larger asset mix.

5C.4 Preference Shares

These are a halfway house between ordinary shares and corporate bonds, they offer high and stable income with relative safety, making them a worthwhile home for investors seeking inflation-beating income with little risk of a missed payment or default.

Though they stand behind all corporate debt in insolvency, they rank ahead of ordinary shares. This is true for dividends too, so no ordinary dividend can be paid until preferred holders have been reimbursed. Dividends on preferred shares are cumulative, so where any dividend may have been unpaid in a previous year, solvent companies usually make up payments eventually.

I currently hold the preference shares of Lloyds Bank 9.75% (LLPD). The price of these shares has increased significantly in recent years as the economic recovery takes hold and the stability of the banking system appears more secure - the shares currently (Feb 2018) yield around 5.5%.

.

5C.5 FTSE ORB Index

The London Stock Exchange's electronic Order book for Retail Bonds (ORB) was launched in 2013 in response to growing private investor demand for easier access to trading bonds.

ORB offers electronic trading in gilts and retail-size corporate bonds, i.e. those which are tradable in smaller, more manageable denominations of £1,000 or similar. These include some of the UK's most well-known companies such as Vodafone, GlaxoSmithKline, BT and Marks & Spencer.

It also provides corporate issuers with an efficient mechanism for distributing bonds to private investors –

helping to stimulate new issues of bonds that are tradable in smaller denominations and providing private investors.

Most useful to investors is possibly the FTSE ORB Total Return Index, which computes the return with the price performance and interest payments of each bond within the universe, and the Gross Redemption Yield with wider investment opportunities.

For those interested in retail bonds visit the London Stock Exchange site - http://www.londonstockexchange.com/traders-and-brokers/security-types/retail-bonds/lse-bonds/retail-bonds-microsite.htm

5.D Exchange Traded Funds & Index Trackers

Index Funds or Trackers have become very popular with the small investor in recent years, myself included, and now account for around 14% of the private investor market.

For those investors who decide to sidestep direct shares and/or investment trusts in favour of a more passive approach using low cost trackers, I will give a brief outline of the sort of approach I may use.

The big attraction of this strategy is that it is low cost, fairly easy to understand and simple to implement.

The largest provider of both index funds and ETFs is **Vanguard** with assets under management of over $5 trillion so a good starting point for research is their UK website www.vanguardinvestor.co.uk

Select the "What We Offer" tab. From the Index and Active Funds on offer, the obvious candidates to explore would be their FTSE UK Equity Income fund, Global Equity Income, Global Corp. Bond Index and their UK Investment Grade Bond.

From the ETF offerings, they have their FTSE All World High Dividend Yield, also FTSE Developed Asia Pacific ETF - also, their FTSE 100 ETF.

For those income investor requiring a natural yield, the main item of interest is the FTSE All World High Dividend Yield (VHYL). The index consists of over 1000 higher yielding large and mid-cap companies listed all around the world. The largest sector of 35% is USA followed by UK 10%, Japan 6%, Switzerland 6% - also France, Canada, Germany, Australia, China and Brazil.

The current yield (Jan 2018) is 3.0% and the income is distributed on a quarterly basis. The annual costs are very competitive at just 0.29% TER.

Vanguard LifeStrategy

These were launched in June 2011 and comprise of a family of five ready-made blended portfolios which have each been professionally constructed from Vanguard's underlying index funds - some equity and some bonds. The LS range offers instant diversification, automatic rebalancing and low costs - ongoing charges of 0.22%.

The natural yield of around 1.4% would mean they could be ignored by many seekers of a higher natural yield. This would be a mistake in my humble opinion. I believe any low cost investment fund which can deliver a reasonable return is worthy of consideration, as it will always be an option for the income seeker to sell down some of the units in a fund, say at the end of each year, to deliver the equivalent e.g. 4% 'income'.

The return on my holding, LifeStrategy 60 (60% equities/40% bonds) has been over 9% per year since launch in 2011 so easily covering my required income of 4% p.a. I am not suggesting this will be the norm every year and I expect the figure to reduce in time to nearer 6% or 7% which would be closer to the longer term average for such a mix of equities and bonds.

The average annualised return for each level of LS fund to end 2017 are as follows:

LifeStrategy 20   6.4% p.a.

LifeStrategy 40   7.8% p.a.

LifeStrategy 60   9.2% p.a.

LifeStrategy 80   10.5% p.a.

LifeStrategy100   11.7% p.a.

Another large provider of exchange traded funds is **Blackrock iShares** http://www.ishares.com/uk/ - the first port of call should be their **Education** section which provides an overview of the products offered, the basics of using an index approach as well as the important consideration of costs and asset allocation.

After a short period, it should be possible to create a shortlist of ETFs - whether equities, bonds, emerging markets or property - which will deliver the level of desired income from the wide and diverse range on offer.

Some iShares I currently hold or have held or researched in recent years are iShares £ Corporate Bond (SLXX), also the ex financials version (ISXF), iShares UK Dividend (IUKD), iShares UK Gilts (IGLT) and their index linked version (INXG), iShares Euro Dividend (IDVY) and iShares Asia Pacific Dividend (IAPD)

Dividend Aristocrats

One further option to consider in the world of ETFs of interest to the income investor is the range of dividend aristocrats offered by State Street SPDR
http://www.spdrseurope.com/index.seam

They have a range of trackers - global, UK, Euro and S&P 500 which track the respective index which follows only those higher dividend yielding companies which meet certain criteria. For example, the S&P Global Dividend Aristocrats is designed to measure the performance of the highest dividend yielding companies within the S&P Global Broad Market Index (BMI) that have followed a policy of increasing or stable dividends for at least 10 consecutive years. The ticker for this is GBDV and the yield (Dec 2017) was 4.5% and TER 0.45%.

The UK tracker (UKDV) provides a yield of 3.8% (again Dec 2017) and has a slightly lower TER of 0.30%. The S&P UK High Yield Dividend Aristocrats Index is designed to measure the performance of the 30 highest dividend-yielding UK companies within the S&P Europe Broad Market Index (BMI), as determined in accordance with the Index methodology, that have followed a managed dividends policy of increasing or stable dividends for at least 10 consecutive years.

These aristocrat ETFs are certainly worthy of consideration - the UK version was launched in February 2012.

The above are just some of the options to consider and are provided as a possible starting point for research - other providers are listed at the end of this book

5.E Multi-Asset Funds

To some, perhaps many, the prospect of deciding on the best approach to investing for income outlined above will be daunting so anything which can make the process easier is to be welcomed. We have seen in an earlier chapter how it's important to find the right mix of assets to match your risk profile and temperament and also the importance of a diverse portfolio. You then have a vast number of options to sift through and when you are settled on you selection there will be the possibility of rebalancing at regular intervals. Welcome to the world of DIY investing.

However, it does not need to be so complex as you can choose to go for one (or more) multi-asset (or multi-index) funds where a manager holds a large mix of different assets in one fund and will vary the content from time to time. For this service you will pay a fee of between 0.2% and 1.25% depending on the type of fund selected.

As we have seen earlier, Vanguard Lifestrategy falls into this category - they are a multi-**index** fund with low charges of 0.22% and hold a mix of equities and bonds. They are classified as a 'passive' fund as there is no manager.

There are many more actively managed multi-**asset** funds and one of the best places to research these is Trustnet's - **Multi Manager and Mixed Assets** section

https://www2.trustnet.com/Investments/MultiManagerMixed Asset.aspx?univ=O

The mixed investment funds are classified according to level of equities and broadly correspond to cautious, balanced and adventurous - so, lowest equities would be 0 - 35% shares, then medium 20% - 60% shares and finally higher equities 40% to 85% shares. There is also a 'flexible' section where the fund manager has a wider remit to hold whatever mix is felt appropriate.

If fund yield is the most important criteria then just click on the 'yield' column to sort from high to low. If total return is more important then sort by 1yr, 3yr or 5yr returns.

Unfortunately there is no filter for ongoing charges so it will be necessary to click on the fund name to load further information.

5.4 Setting an Alert

Individual shares, Investment Trusts or ETFs on your shortlist which have not yet been purchased should be kept under review. Weakness in share price or a downturn of sentiment towards a sector can mean a more favourable yield is on offer.

One of the useful facilities with some sites such as Interactive Investor and Trustnet is the 'Alert' tool with which you can ask the broker to email you if any particular share or IT/ETF falls (or rises) to a set price. It could be that one of your selections has a current yield of 3.5% and share price of 200p. The dividend per share is therefore 7.0p for the whole year. You would prefer to purchase with a higher yield of say 4.0%. If you set the alert for a price of 175p, this would be sufficient to provide the desired higher yield. Should the share or IT/ETF price fall below the desired target price in the weeks or months to come, you will be automatically alerted via email. You do not need to watch every share or trust on the watchlist every day!

5.4 Summary

Whether you decide to select individual shares, or use investment trusts, funds or the all-in-one multi-asset funds will be a matter for personal preference. Many will opt for investments which can deliver a natural yield but some will consider the simple, lower cost index funds or ETFs and focus on total return.

There is no right or wrong strategy, the key to success will be to settle on a diversified, low cost portfolio which you can hold for the long term. To do this you will need to find the right mix of assets which mesh with your attitude to risk and with your personality.

If you are naturally cautious, you probably will not be suited to the higher volatility from a portfolio of individual shares. The level of equities to bonds and possibly property selected to provide your income should always revolve around the type of person you are and what risk you are prepared to accept when the markets head south. At the start you may think you would be relaxed with a 10% dip in the markets but you will not actually know until the event happens.

Investing, whether for income or otherwise is all about staying the course for the long haul and therefore adopting a sensible asset allocation to withstand whatever the ups and downs the markets will deliver.

6. Monitor Your Portfolio

Although the aim is long term buy and hold, it will be necessary to review the portfolio on a regular basis - maybe every 6 or 12 months. Some assets will perform more strongly than others at certain times. If left totally to its own devices, your portfolio will most likely become unbalanced over a period of time.

The reason for a periodic review is to check that it still fulfils its purpose of balancing risk and reward. From time to time, as we have seen, it will be necessary to rebalance your portfolio to restore your preferred equity/bond ratio according to your investment plan - this is normally done once per year.

For example, if you decide upon a mix of 40% equities and 60% bonds, over time this will get out of kilter as the equities rise or fall. If the equities do well one year you may find your portfolio becomes nearer 50:50 so to maintain the portfolio at the level of risk you desire, it will be important to sell off 10% of the equities and reinvest this surplus into bonds.

Remember that investing for the long-term means trying your best to tune out the market noise; too often headlines can trick us into making badly-timed, or emotional, decisions that may prove to be detrimental in the long term.

Some investors believe 'long term buy & hold' means 'never sell'. Whilst this may be the intention when the purchase is made, there may be circumstances when it may be necessary to take some form of action - this is probably far more like with an individual shares portfolio than with collectives.

Occasionally the market will offer you a genuinely inflated price for your shares - possibly double what you paid - at which time it becomes a question a comparison between holding that share versus others being offered at a more reasonable price/higher yield whilst not compromising the quality of the income stream. If you are capable of assessing whether a share is a buy, you are probably capable of assessing when it is a sell.

As time passes, some shares will do well, others may struggle depending on market cycles and other factors. Obviously if the share price rises significantly on one or two holdings in your portfolio, the dividend yield (which is a proportion of the price) will fall so the question may arise as to what happens if a share's yield falls well below the market average.

If this is due to the company **ceasing to pay dividends** completely, with little prospect of resumption - this was the case with some banks after the dramatic events of 2008 - then there may be a case for selling the holding and recycling the proceeds into a better share. Hopefully, such events will not be repeated too often and it is far more likely the fall in yield is merely down to a substantial rise in share price.

In this situation then you have to balance the rate at which dividends are increasing with the return on your capital indicated by the yield. In certain situations, it may be appropriate to **top slice** a holding which has raced ahead of others - sell say 25% of the shares and recycle the proceeds into another higher yielding holding and thereby restore more of an even balance to the income stream. You probably do not want to find your portfolio has become seriously unbalanced and where, for example, over 50% of the income is generated by 5 or 6 shares in your 20 share portfolio.

Some people may wish to track their portfolio via the likes of Trustnet Portfolio which allow you to set up one or more portfolios, mixing asset classes if desired as well as different styles of strategy.

https://www2.trustnet.com/Tools/

So, in summary, as a general rule "tinkering" with the portfolio should be avoided although from time to time, it may be necessary to take some action to maintain a broad balance of the income stream.

6.1 Keeping Track of Dividend Income

So far as dividends are concerned, you will need to keep a record of what is due from each company. I have created a simple spreadsheet which lists all the investments I hold and all the dividends due throughout the year. Individual shares normally pay twice per year in the form of an interim and a final dividend. With many investment trusts it is more common for quarterly dividends.

As new information becomes available - dividend announcements etc., I update the spreadsheet and therefore have a reasonable idea of how much income to expect in any particular month and importantly, can instantly see the projected income for the whole year. Check to see the expected dividends and other income has actually been received in your online account shortly after the due date.

It will possible involve a little work initially to set up the spreadsheet but I believe it is well worth the effort. Once established and up and running, it should not take a lot of time to input the various updated figures. Of course, one years spreadsheet can be used for the following year using the "save as.." facility.

6.2 Keeping Track of Capital

As with income, it will be useful to maintain a separate spreadsheet to record your Investments, date of purchase, price paid and current capital return (e.g. share price increase). It does not need to be a complex affair but it can be useful to monitor the weight of different assets as an aid to rebalancing - for example between fixed income and equities.

For further details, I have provided an outline of both customised spreadsheets (income/capital) in articles on my blog.

If you would prefer to a ready-made tool, there are several brokers who offer a portfolio tracking facility, this may work just fine for just a handful of different investments but for those with more than half a dozen, it may be worth looking at some of the facilities (free) such as with Trustnet or Morningstar - the latter is possibly the more powerful and offers various options such as an overall snapshot, performance graph which includes figures for returns of several years on an annualised basis.

Which ever method you choose, the main thing is to select a system that suits you and which will provide you with the information you need to effectively manage your portfolio. Try not to over complicate the situation with unnecessary information.

Investegate

To monitor news, results, dividend declarations etc on either your current portfolio or investments on your watch list, I find it very useful to register (free)
with www.investegate.co.uk

You can then add your selected shares, investment trusts or ETFs to an "alerts" list. You can choose to have all announcements emailed to you or just particular announcements such as results or dividend announcements.

For funds, use the FE Trustnet fundswire facility.

7. Conclusion

In this brief introduction to DIY Income, I have attempted to provide an outline of the various ways it is possible to generate a little more income from savings, maybe an inheritance or pension lump sum. This may be relevant to some people approaching retirement having regard to the changes to pension liberation which came into force in April 2015. I have also described some of the methods I have personally used over recent years to generate income from my own portfolios (Stocks & Shares ISA and SIPP Drawdown) - mainly using investment trusts and index funds.

Of course, there are many different ways to approach this - I have become accustomed to my particular style of using these investments methods. When I started 25 years previously, such vehicles as trackers and exchange traded funds had not been invented - for that matter nor had the internet!

Investment trusts are just one tried and tested method I have found to work for me and which, over the long term, should continue to provide above-inflation tax-free returns which will supplement my state pension in later years. More recently I have introduced index funds - Vanguard Lifestrategy 60 is my largest portfolio holding and because it offers less natural income, I find other creative ways to take the 'income' I require.

The stock market has been rising in recent years and accordingly, the capital value of the investments I made some years ago have also risen. The overall dividend yield on my portfolio is currently around 4.0% which means for every £1,000 invested, my return is £40 per year. The overall growth on my mixed portfolio including dividends has seen an average of around 8% p.a. over the past 9 years - well ahead of current inflation rates. I try to take an income of around 4% each year and leave the rest invested as a reserve.

This contrasts to the returns from my building society - currently 1.4% which means for every £1,000 saved, my annual interest is £14 - of course there is no risk to the capital and volatility is zero. Also my savings are protected under the government compensation scheme AND there is speculation the rates may start to rise in 2018!

Investing is by no means suitable for everyone as I hope I have made clear earlier in the book. If some people have come to the end of this book and have reached the conclusion that the approach of DIY Income is not for them, that is absolutely fine. **It is not the aim of this book to persuade anyone to invest on the stock market - merely to provide information, options and the (dubious) benefit of my personal experience**.

For those who decide they want to give it a go - again fine but be sure you fully understand what you are doing and remember, its not a race and its not a competition - if you are new to investing, start off with a small proportion of your hard-earned savings and see how it goes. Take it slow and steady, dip a toe in the water and see how it feels - if the first year goes according to plan, add a little more.

For me, successful investing is never a completed task but more a continual learning process - for example, in 2015 I reviewed my investment strategy and have sold off my shares portfolio and moved to embrace index funds, particularly the Vanguard LifeStrategy upon which my latest book '**DIY Simple Investing**' is based.

Income can be just the natural yield from an investment but can also be taken from capital growth - nothing is set in stone.

Finally - everyone makes mistakes, particularly at the start of the investing journey and which is to be expected. Try to learn where you may have gone wrong.

I think if you get to the stage where you are making more good decisions than poor ones, you are likely to be on the right track. Experience combined with the ability to keep an open mind counts for a great deal when it comes to investing as with many other areas of life, so do whatever you need to do to learn from every mistake you make – and then try not repeat them!

Some investors like to maintain a journal to records their decisions, random thoughts and everything else to do with their investing journey. If your memory is not so good then that could in itself be the best investment you ever make.

Good luck!

                Copyright © 2018 John Edwards

Some useful websites

My Own Blog
www.diyinvestoruk.blogspot.co.uk

Other Useful Blogs
www.monevator.com (passive index)
www.retirementinvestingtoday.com
www.awealthofcommonsense.com

Online Brokers
www.h-l.co.uk
www.youinvest.co.uk
www.cavendishonline.co.uk
www.halifax.co.uk/sharedealing/
www.alliancetrustsavings.co.uk
www.charles-stanley-direct.co.uk

Research
www.digitallook.com
www.theaic.co.uk
www.trustnet.com
www.morningstar.co.uk
www.fixedincomeinvestments.org.uk
www.upcomingdividends.co.uk

Product Providers (Collective Investments)
www.vanguardinvestor.co.uk
www.ishares.com/uk/individual/en/index.page
www.etf.hsbc.com
www.legalandgeneral.com/investments/products-and-funds/index-tracker/
www.spdrseurope.com/index.seam
www.henderson.com/

Community
www.moneysavingexpert.com

Other
www.citywire.co.uk
www.thisismoney.co.uk

My Other Books

'DIY Introduction to Personal Finance'
'DIY Pensions'
'DIY Simple Investing'

Printed in Great Britain
by Amazon

more recently I have found that looking after a portfolio of 25 shares was taking up more time and also I became a little uncomfortable with the constant volatility.

I have therefore adjusted my strategy and adopted a combination of investment trusts and low cost index funds. The latter provide the additional diversification of the all-in-one feature of global equities and bonds in one holding.

One important criteria is the level of income required from the capital/savings you have to invest. With the Bank of England reducing the bank rate to 0.5% since 2009 and with corresponding savings rates at an all time low - around 1.0% to 2% or so - some investors may be happy to target a starting yield of 3% or 4% on equities/bonds with the intention to grow the dividend income ahead of inflation. Others may want to push the boat out in the early years with a more aggressive target of, say 4.5% - 5% knowing they have other streams of income to come in the years ahead e.g. maturing policy or company pension etc.

However each individual will need to decide on their own approach - some may favour holding just individual shares accepting the greater degree of volatility, others may be happy to use collectives such as a simple passive index approach or invest for income via investment trusts or multi-asset funds - there really is no one size fits all!

Everyone's attitude to risk, diversification, income needs etc. will differ so this is very much a personal choice in terms of what works best for you as an individual investor - only you can know what balance feels comfortable, indeed it may take some time investing using an assortment of methods before this can be fully determined.

The following is a detailed step-by step guide to how I personally have approached the process of selecting the investments I have most knowledge and experience about - individual shares, investment trusts, fixed interest securities, ETFs and index tracker funds and finally, Multi-Asset funds.